# YOUNG VIC TAKING PA

## Three Plays by Luke Barnes

Men In Blue

Fable

The Jumper Factory

OBERON BOOKS
LONDON

WWW.OBERONBOOKS.COM

First published in 2018 by Oberon Books Ltd
521 Caledonian Road, London N7 9RH
Tel: +44 (0) 20 7607 3637 / Fax: +44 (0) 20 7607 3629
e-mail: info@oberonbooks.com
www.oberonbooks.com

A catalogue record for this book is available from the British
Library.

PB ISBN: 9781786825803
E ISBN: 9781786825810

Cover: image by S-BELOV, design by Young Vic Taking Part

Printed and bound by 4edge Limited, Essex, UK.
eBook conversion by Lapiz Digital Services, India.

# Contents

## Foreword

We're all conceived and born and find our feet in the world in more or less the same way. We're all vulnerable to hunger and cold, to desire, disgust, despair.

All our bodies come equipped with minds that struggle to persuade, instruct, encourage, insist that our bodies damn well behave in the way we want them to!

And we all have minds surrounded by bodies through whose suppleness, tenderness, sensitivity, strength they receive zillions of units of information per nano-second – forming them, shaping them, seducing them, educating them.

We're all the same. How then can one person's experience be considered of greater value than that of any other human being?

We're all bursting at the seams with our need to express what we think about the world and how we feel about sharing our lives with each other. We seem to be hard-wired to tell stories. There's nothing we can do about it. Whether our stories are true or inventions, we can't stop telling them – to ourselves and to each other.

But some of us feel entitled to tell our stories and others don't. Why should that be?

Professional actors and writers train over years – or decades, or over their whole lives – to be able to tell many different stories about many different characters and situations. The best of them are also always talking about themselves.

But everyone has a story to tell – about how they came into the world … and where … and when they first noticed themselves … and who was there when that happened … and why it happened as it did… and whether it mattered or it didn't … and what happened next.

Listening to those stories told with all the deep power of the human heart, we all add hugely to our own experience of what it means to be living today.

The Young Vic Taking Part team enable those stories to be told – about us, to us, in our own presence and in the presence of those who matter to us most.

And so we become more fully ourselves. Nothing matters more.

It was my great joy at the Young Vic – and the joy too of hundreds of the theatre artists I worked with over my time – to stand or sit and listen and, in that way, take part in the life affirming achievements of the Taking Part Team.

Long may they continue. I am certain they will.

**David Lan**
**Artistic Director**
**Young Vic**
**2000–2018**

## The Function Of Art

Humans started telling stories around camp fires with a very simple purpose: To share stories in the hope that the world would become easier for others. Since those days the world has changed but our reasons for telling stories stay the same. We tell stories with an intention. Whether it be to get people to see the world, to turn away from it, or to make others feel less alone all story telling has to have an intention in its telling. These plays exist with intention. They have been written for a reason. They are not vehicles for fame. They are not vanity projects. They are not a demonstration of intelligence. They exist clearly within the parameter of their purpose. *Men In Blue* exists to give community to men who are service users with the NHS for mental wellbeing, *Fable* exists as a platform to share their experiences of migration and reimagine the narrative to challenge the popular conception from a lived perspective and *The Jumper Factory* exists, in the first instance, for a performance in prison to help men articulate their emotional lives in a world where emotional life isn't discussed and in the second as a deterrent for young people at risk of offending. When we talk of making Theatre we have to talk about the *reason* for putting a show on in the parameters of the place, time and space of each production with the absence of the ego of the writer, director, or actors. What is important is the gesture of making this thing, here, now, what that signifies and what the repercussions of the act of doing that thing are. This is Theatre with a function as all Theatre should be. If you are a maker of Theatre, a story teller, or indeed anyone who does *anything* I hope that you take from this that every venture we set out to do must have an intention and that intention has to transcend ego, money making, or career advancement. Everything we do has to have an intention and hope of change within in it in this time and space; with these people.

The act of putting the bodies of people, that aren't actors but look and sound like me and you, telling their true stories is the purest form of Theatre imaginable. We learn from doing this that beyond the intelligent forms, and star actors, and politics of British Theatre there are lives being lived that are so close to our own both in physical proximity and potential futures. We learn that we are all born into this world the same and it's our experiences that shape us. We learn through looking at each other's experiences and lives how we live our own. We learn to understand the complexities of human existence and we learn, through drama, to empathise with those complexities. As we learn to empathise we learn to be better humans and make choices in our relationships, our businesses, in our Art, that make life easier for others. The urgency of storytelling goes beyond the politics of Art. What this collection of plays offers is a by-pass from agents, ego-driven actors, politics and cuts to the main function of Art: to share the human experience so we may grow to be human beings more understanding of each other, of the self, of the society and of the landscape we exist in. We do not need anything other than truth to tell stories. There is a point to making Theatre and is it not in ego, it is not in fame, it is not in recognition but in the simple act of a group of men sharing their experiences with mental wellbeing to other men experiencing the same to feel less alone. It is in prisoners exploring their emotional lives with other men in a way they never would have been able to in day to day life. It is in migrants telling their stories to debunk the narrative we are told by popular media. That is the tangible social value of Art. It is as simple as that. And for every simple truth we tell with intention and the hope of a repercussion on a particular audience we cure the infection audiences catch from hammy Shakespeares, from over-clever new plays, from live art that thrives off its own complexities and elitism. This is the simple truth and in engaging with it we grow as individuals, as friends, as children, as parents, as lovers, as communities, as societies and as a species. That is the *function* of Art.

What I hope that these plays demonstrate is the irrevocable bond between community and Theatre. That buildings have a responsibility to make Art with a function that is intrinsically linked with the lives and concerns of the people living within its reach. The function of Art must have resonance with the lives of the community the building it's serving. We must be presenting work that is of the community, for the community, and in service of the community the building exists in. When we talk to a community and hear their stories we can begin to make Art with a function for this community, in this place, in this time that is of use of the people that engage with it.

**Luke Barnes 2018**

Taking Part at the Young Vic is at the heart of the work of the theatre. We create projects and shows inspired by the productions on our main stages with our neighbours in Lambeth and Southwark. We want everyone in our local area to feel welcome and that the Young Vic is for them. In this collection you can read work we made with men with mental health issues, with school children around the world and with men incarcerated in our criminal justice system. This is a window into the plays we create, amongst many more, with many more people. Taking Part is one of the ways we keep our doors wide open. Come on in.

**Imogen Brodie**
**Director of Taking Part**

**The Young Vic is supported by:**

**Young Vic Taking Part would like to thank**
The 29th May 1961 Charitable Trust, Andor Charitable Trust, Lisa and Adrian Binks, Garfield Western Foundation, The Golden Bottle Trust, The Harold Hyam Wingate Foundation, Isango Ensemble, The Limbourne Trust, Chris and Jane Lucas, Paul Hamlyn Foundation, Richard Radcliffe Charitable Trust, The Sackler Trust.

*"For the people of Lambeth and Southwark"*

**MEN IN BLUE**

Written by Luke Barnes, developed with the company
Directed by Finn den Hertog

*Men in Blue* was a Young Vic Taking Part Community Production inspired by *Blue/Orange*.

It was first performed at Platform Southwark on 15 July 2016, and at the Latitude Festival on 17 July 2016.

In 2016 the Young Vic staged *Blue/Orange* by Joe Penhall. Set in a psychiatric hospital, the play deals with the struggle between two doctors over what to do with a young patient, who claims that oranges are blue.

In response, we wanted to create a project that brought the voices of the 'patients' to the fore, in particular men, who are disproportionately affected by mental health problems. We worked with Lambeth Early Onset SLAM and St Thomas' Hospital to bring together a group of men with experience of a variety of conditions, including depression, psychosis and schizophrenia, to work with writer Luke Barnes and director Finn den Hertog.

The *Men in Blue* project was an opportunity for this group of men to talk – to each other, to us and to you – about themselves. About how they might feel right now, about how they have felt in the past, about how they deal with the world today and about how they feel about being a man, and through that, for Luke to create a story from the material we gathered. Some of the words in the play are taken directly from various writing exercises, some from interviews and some based on Luke's observations. When we gave the script to the participants to read and respond to, one phrase kept coming up: *"This sounds like my life."*

We hope that you will recognise the honesty and strength that has gone into creating *Men in Blue*. And we hope that we all keep talking.

**Kirsten Adam**
**Two Boroughs Project Manager**

**Creative Team**

| | |
|---|---|
| Director and Dramaturg | Finn den Hertog |
| Two Boroughs Project Manager | Kirsten Adam |
| Director of Taking Part | Imogen Brodie |

**Company**

| | |
|---|---|
| Billy | James |
| Gary | Jose |
| Gbenga | Josh |
| Hristo | Ruaridh |

**With special thanks to:**

David, Dennis, Jonathan, Joseph, Maciej, Malachai, Umaru, Ed McFadden, Jide Ashimi, Olivia Rowe, St Thomas's Hospital, Lambeth Early Onset Team, the *Blue/Orange* Cast and Company, and all at the Young Vic.

## 1. Worried About Your Well Being

You're worried about your well being.
You're at work. You're empty.
You're standing watching everyone else go about their business
Your eyes are focused on a discount offer on Wotsits
The packaging of Wotsits seeps into you
The cheerfulness pisses you off
The optimism of orange balanced against coughing up Wotsits dust.
You think about the girl from school who had skin like Wotsits.
You remember how she tried to make you finger her a bit after P.E and you said no because you thought that her flaps might flake off.
You'd kill for that now.
You think that maybe if you knew someone wanted you to finger them you wouldn't feel so bad.
You see the people walk past.
You notice how weird people are
You notice how there are a lot of really attractive women with really average men
You think there's hope for you yet
If you could hold a conversation
If you didn't feel like this.
And that was when you knew you weren't the same as everyone else
That moment where you blamed yourself for being alone.
At least you thought no one else felt like this.
You never thought this would be you.
You never thought you would feel this bad.
You're at home watching Deal or No Deal
You're sitting in that chair
The one you sit in sometimes to get some distance between you and your mum
Your mum is sitting on the couch.
The smell of your mum's cigarette drifts to your nose
You realise how much her smoking has always pissed you off.
On the screen Noel Edmunds is pulling faces at red boxes

You wonder if he knows that goatees are shit and that the
whole world thinks he's a paedo.
You worry your mum is thinking she fucked you up
You know she didn't but there's every chance she's thinking that.
You don't want to talk because you know she's going to ask
you why you're being quiet
You don't want people to make you talk
You just want everything to carry on
You know that this is bringing you closer
But it feels like it's further away.
You hope that she will ease her way into it over time.
Because it is killing you.

## 2. What It Feels Like

Like a weeping willow
Like a ticking clock
Like shadows on the wall
Like an empty playground
Like ashes
Like melted cheese
Like the air on a Monday morning
Like body odour
Like salt water tears
Like sand paper
Like quicksand
Like sinking
Like suffocating
Like sour sweets
Like bitter
Like blackness
Like burnt food
Liker vertigo
Like vinegar
Like vomit
Like porridge
Like prison doors
Like crying
Like screaming
Like deafening silence
Like ketchup
Like wotsits
Like cigarette smoke
Like Noel Edmunds

## 3. Standing By An A Road

You find yourself standing by an A Road.
You think about what it would be like if you stepped into the
80 mile an hour traffic
You think about the ease
The release of the weight
The end of people judging you
People watching you
All your problems seem easily answerable
They all seem
Simple.
All you have to do is put one of your feet in front of the other
And let a car smash into the side of you
Your brain will stop
Your mind will silence
And there will be nothing left but the bliss of not feeling
The escape from the weight.
It seems logical.

You think about Noel Edmonds
You think about Deal or No Deal
You think about your mother
How you always watch it together
You picture her face as she see's your body on the ground
Her standing in a morgue looking at your head with half a face
You think about her being alone
And telling her friends

And her friends sitting next to each other as she does what
you're doing now
Staring into nothing.
It makes you feel guilty.
You can't want to do that to her.
You turn around
And you walk away

## 4. A Man Is

A man is a fool
A man is dumb
A man is heavy built and hard being
A man is being vulnerable
A man is one of many brothers
A man is a mere mortal
A man is his own best friend
A man is not an island
A man is competitive
A man is ugly
A man is at the mercy of women
A man is strong
A man is bold
A man is alpha
A man doesn't always know what it means to be a man unless someone tells him
A man is not the opposite of a woman
A man is not what you expect a man to be.
A man feels
A man doesn't know if a man should feel
A man is stereotypical.
A man is doomed
A man is a survivor

## 5. The Doctor

You're in the waiting room.
You think everyone is staring at you guessing what's wrong.
They're probably not.
You're not thinking logically.
The doctor comes in and reads your name like a machine.
In his office you sit in a chair
It's metallic and standard issue.
He sits opposite you.
The look in his eye is, at the same time, both quite loving and
a bit doubtful.
Sort of like he's been here before a thousand times and he's
met a thousand yous.
You think you're not like him.
You can see by his shirt, that slightly arrogant smile, the flick
in his hair that you're not like him. He's from a different world
and already
There's something in between you
A divide of culture?
Something.

He looks right in your eye
And he asks you:

**DOCTOR**     What's the matter?

You tell him what happened
You tell him about the tears in the toilets
The staring
The emptiness
About the feeling of not wanting to exist
About thinking that everyone would be better if you were dead
About that fact you're an alien inside your own body.

He smiles
Thinking he knows your mind better than you.

**DOCTOR**     We all get like this – being human is a verb, not
               a noun. It's just a matter of remembering to do
               things. You might need a little push.

You ask him what it would take to be under observation in hospital

**DOCTOR**     Are you going to hurt yourself?

You think about it

…No

You can't stop thinking about your mother

**DOCTOR**     Are you going to hurt anyone else?

No.

The fact he's asking means he doesn't understand.

**DOCTOR**     Good because we don't have beds.
              Not worth it anyway.
              Worst case scenario is that you forget how to live
              if you're here too long
              You need to deal with the world
              You need to learn to live
              Life is a gift
              And I'm here to help.

He writes on a bit of paper

**DOCTOR**     Here you go

You're amazed how easy that was.
You're amazed he didn't examine you
You just told him things.
You're amazed that you could have been lying and been put on life long medication.
You start to wonder whether you could make money selling prescription medicine on the streets.

You ask him if it's possible you can have a yeast infection as a male
You don't care
You just want to feel better.

## 7. What If?

On the bus home you start to think:

There was no talk of ever coming off the medicine.
No way of being told what to do next.
Do you just take them forever?
Is this what you are now?
A body full of chemicals?
What if they wear off?
What if you become resistant?
You stand and stare.
And you feel people stare at you
Like they know about you.
Like they know what's going on in your head.
What are you supposed to do now?
Why does no one tell you what to do now?

## 8. A Conversation Between You And Your Younger Self

A Conversation Between You And Your Younger Self

Nothing will happen to me

Maybe it won't.

Everything's going to be fine.

Maybe.

Wait! If something does happen?

If it does
Remember that it passes
Everything passes.

How can I stop it though?
You can't.
How can I make it better?
Don't overthink things
Think for yourself
Question everything

Follow your dreams and ambitions

…Express yourself?

Try to empathise with people

Learn from your mistakes

Don't be too worried about what other people think

Don't take yourself too seriously

There is more to life than materialistic things

A healthy life is a balanced one

Don't be afraid to speak your mind about what you truly think

Take the rough with the smooth

Stay around good people

Don't put all your faith in women
Or men
Try and do something you enjoy whilst looking forward to
something else you enjoy
Exercise
Know that everyone else's mind is chaos too

Speak up.
There are tons of people who will say I know what you're
talking about
There are tons of people who want to help you.
And never forget the need to love.

And remember it passes and you want to love
Everything passes.

Everything passes.

## 9. Two Versions Of The Truth

The good book speaks to me in volumes.

I want to bring some positivity into this darkness that is
devouring me.

It's like Chinese whispers, sometimes the whispers get twisted.

I have an epiphany so vivid and so real that it's driving me doolally

I don't know whether it was the Devil himself, or demons

I can hear suffering and mourning and screaming.

Connotations from Revelation got me anxious

Everyone from my past, my present and my future fighting
this war.

I'm breaking down on a train.
The colours are warning me where to go.

I can't read.
I trade my mental faculties for divine revelations.
I need to follow the calling, find some help.
Light pours out of my eyes, manifesting a brighter world.

I'm making deals with Civil Servants in my head.
I'm like Atlas, I need to think of how to hold up the world.

The need for food, sleep and rest dissolve in side of me.
My mind becomes open to the secrets of the universe.

I glimpse a version of humanity that could work.
I feel sure of our purpose:

To safeguard the weak.

## 10. You're Managing

When people ask you, you say that you're managing.
You recognise the main thing is loneliness
And everything that comes with it.

You try to fit in
You go to functions
You go to events

But you know it's hard.
The future is unknown
You say to yourself you live one day at a time

Take the medication
Hope it doesn't come again
Keep yourself too busy to think about tomorrow.

You wonder whether medicine is good
Or whether you're just supposed to feel like this.

You feel like a burden on your mother
You worry that she's going off the deep end

You worry that she's going off the end and she's holding it all
together for you.
Your mother see's you as a problem. A burden

You worry that her life
Her coffee mornings

Her trips to the pub
Her chats with her friends

Are all about you
Or at least if there not about you in words

They're about you in her head.
Everything she does is now about you think

And it bothers you.
You feel that her life would be better without you.

You just want to make things easier for her

You think about moving out.
You talk to her for hours
She tells you she loves you

You don't believe her
You can't believe anyone could love you
You can't believe that anyone could love what you are now

So you leave.

## 11. Today Is

Today is my only chance of living
Today is all that I have
Today is when I remember the life I lived
Today is when I think of the future
Today is match day
Today is only reality
Today is crazy day.

## 12. Your New Life

It's the first day of your new life
You're in your new flat
Miles away from anywhere you know
Nowhere near Mum
Or work
Or school
It's the third floor of a tower block
Grey
Tall
Standing alone looking out over the city

You can't see fuck all
But it *does* look out over the city.
Single glazed windows
Thin doors
Groups of people hanging around.
You're scared of getting robbed
You know there's nothing to rob
You don't trust people
You think all the groups of people are planning to rob you.
You're extra careful when you leave.

You think about buying a dog.
A big black one that scares people
But it scares you
The idea of having a dog rip off your face is terrifying.
You realise the irony of this is quite funny.
You worry that you're getting kicked out because you know
you can't hold down a job. You know that the money from the
job centre won't pay your rent and bills
You're scared.
And because you're scared it makes the feeling worse
It sets in.

## 13. Scared

You're scared of getting worse
You're scared you'll never work.
You're scared you'll be alone forever.
You're scared no one will be able to love you because of this.
You're scared that that when you look at people thinking
they're talking about you, they might be
You're scared that they might be thinking you're weird or worse
You're scared they might be plotting against you
You're still scared you can't make relationships
You're still scared you can't hold down a job.
You're scared you'll never have a family.
You're scared you'll never move on.
And you're scared that what you're most scared of is coming
back.

## 14. Wotsit Girl

You start to blame yourself for being the way you are
You walk
The concrete spills out in front of you and the chewing gum
spangled pavements make you feel dirty
You hear a car behind you
You don't really pay much attention
You're not really paying much attention to anything
You hear a voice

**WOTSIT GIRL**  Hiya

It's her
The girl with the wotsit skin

And for a second you wonder if she's been waiting all these
years to ask you to finger her
But she doesn't

She says

**WOTSIT GIRL**  How you been?

And you don't know what to say
You want to say the you you thought you were is gone
You want to say you feel like that person is dead
You want to say you're downtrodden
You want to say you're a victim
You're struggling to survive
You need help
You're lost

You just say that everything's great
I've been working hard

**WOTSIT GIRL**  You still living at your mum's?

No but...

**WOTSIT GIRL**  Are you ok?

And you look at her
And you say

I'm lost.
And you cry.

And you get in her car
And you go to her mum's
And she cooks baked potato with beans
You sit in her front room and they ask you what you've been doing
And you tell them
And you smile

## 15. A Happy(ish) Ending(ish)

Outside you call your mum.
There's not much to say.
You just sit in silence on the phone.
But it brings you some comfort
And you know she doesn't mind.

And in that silence
You realise a cycle.

No work because you're scared of getting ill.
You know the drugs make everything feel it's ok

Underneath you think it's not
You think it's a ticking time bomb.

You don't say anything to your mum.
And after what feels like hours of silence

Hours of just knowing someone is on the phone
Just feeling they're there
Your mum says

**MUM**          I love you you know

And it feels real.

Like the first times you've ever heard anyone say those words
and mean it.

And you know you want to love

You haven't felt that since this all started.

And that's enough for now.

The world turns

The stars shine

And you decide you're going to try and hold on.

**END.**

**FABLE**

Written by Luke Barnes
Directed by Madeleine Kludje

*Fable* was a Young Vic Taking Part Schools Production inspired by Isango Ensemble's *A Man of Good Hope*.

It was created in three parts and first performed by young people at schools in London, New York City and Cape Town between February – April 2017. The film was first screened at The Young Vic in July 2017.

Isango Ensemble is a South African theatre company that draws its artists mainly from the townships around Cape Town. *A Man of Good Hope* told the story of a young refugee who flees Somalia only to discover a new violent life in the townships of South Africa. It was performed at the Young Vic as part of an international tour including South Africa and the USA. The tour took place during the height of the latest refugee crisis in Europe, and at a time when the political situation in each country felt critical.

Following discussions with Isango Ensemble, who were keen to engage with the children in their local township schools, and motivated to improve our local young people's engagement with the circumstances refugees are living in, we took on the challenge of creating work with schools across three continents – to tell a story which felt both universal and personal and would resonate beyond cultural barriers.

*Fable* was written in three parts, designed to travel alongside the central character. Each part tells the same story, but each story is not quite the same. Combined to form a trilogy, *Fable* explores the search for truth in a journey across the globe.

*We were asked to create a piece of theatre telling the truth of immigration. This is the one we are showing. This is my truth.*

*Fable* was written following R&D workshops with young people in London. Our director, Madeleine Kludje, worked closely with Luke to create a story which would feel natural in the voices of our young people without appropriating the real stories of refugees. They were joined by Tristan Shepard, an incredible film maker who made the work we created into a sixty-minute film. Part of this film can be viewed on our blog:

youngviclondon.wordpress.com/2017/09/27/fable-a-story-spanning-three-continents

**Georgia Dale**
**Schools and Colleges Project Manager**

**Creative Team**

Director                                         Madeleine Kludje
Film by                                        Tristan Shepherd
Schools and Colleges Projects Manager    Georgia Dale
Director of Taking Part                     Imogen Brodie
Music and Movement                     Isango Ensemble

**Company**

*Part One: London*

| | |
|---|---|
| Anita | Kelly |
| Anthonia | Mai'da |
| Denver | Pedro |
| Ella | Precious |
| Frank | Rania |
| Jamie | Sharlene |

*Part Two: New York City*

| | |
|---|---|
| Angel | Jermaine |
| Camille | Joel |
| Chanel | Julia |
| Chantelle | Kashe-Liane |
| Christopher | Michaela |
| David | Ty |
| George | Zyhara |
| Giselle | |

*Part Three: Cape Town*

| | |
|---|---|
| Amahle | Namhla |
| Anathi | Nobuhle |
| Anelisiwe | Noluvuyo |
| Anitha | Odwa |
| Asisipho | Onanko |
| Ayabonga | Phielo |
| Esethu | Simamkele |
| Inga | Sinako |
| Ligheme | Sinawo |
| Likhona | Sinovuyo |
| Lingomso | Siphosethu |
| Lisakhanya | Sixolise |
| Lutho | Tshiamo |
| Luyolo | Yakheneni |
| Mihle | Yamkela |

**With special thanks to:**

David Lan, Isango Ensemble, Clare Béjanin, Harris Girls Academy East Dulwich, Sacred Heart Catholic School, Juan Morel Campos Secondary School, McKinney Secondary School of the Arts, Injongo Primary School, Liwa Primary School, Peter Avery at New York State Education Department, Stephen McIntosh and Mikal Lee at Brooklyn Academy of Music, George Young, Good Chance Theatre, Leon Puplett, Sarah Trustman, Heather Osborne, Jemima Robinson

**Note**

The dialogue can be changed in order to fit the mouths and vernacular of the performers.

# Act One

## Prinnyville High School

*A Rehearsal Room. A group of young people are in it.*

*A large whiteboard at the back.*

**1** Why are we in a theatre festival anyway.

**4** Because if we win we get to travel.

**1** Really?

**4** Yeah! It's international. Schools from across the world are doing it. Imagine us – Prinnyville High School going INTERNATIONAL.

*12 comes in.*

**12** I've got the brief from Williamsburg.

**2** What is it?

**12** Okay right so then. The 49th Annual International Schools Theatre Festival. This year. The brief is… We have two weeks to make a show about "The Truth of Immigration"; we have to use a true story as the starting place and then make something theatrical from there.

**4** What we gonna do?

**5** Do any of us know any true stories about immigration?

**6** Shall we look online?

**7** No

**6** Why not?

**7** Because it's not true – it's all clickbait.

**6** Clickbait?

**7** Yeah they just say stuff to get you to click on it and it's not real. Besides EVERYONE will be doing that. The top ten pages on intrasearch will be in everyones plays. We have to do something original. What about Fable?

**6** Fable?

**7** Well we've got to do a real story haven't we. What do you think?

**ALL** …

**9** Well. No one here is an immigrant.

**1** My dad is

**9** Does that make you one?

**1** Kind of.

**9** Alright. Why don't we do one of him then?

**12** That was ages ago. It's all changed now. I think we do a play about Fable.

**6** Why?

**12** She was a foreigner and she was in our class – makes sense. Make's it sound like we're really… heart felt.

**5** Is it fair using someone's life in the hope that we win a competition?

**12** We can say that it's a local story and it has a truthful sort of resonance so that'll be good for the competition.

**5** Yeah but… Morally.

**12** It's based on her and it's not her so that's okay. I think. We just have to try our best to be as accurate as possible and make sure anything we do put in has a bigger truth.

**5** What's a bigger truth?

**12** We're still saying something about immigration even if it's not specific to her. That way this has a point and we're just using Fable as a cornerstone. Okay?

**8** Sounds good to me.

**5** Okay. What have we got so far?

**12** We've got that she was from Sunland.

*They write "From Sunland" on the white board.*

**6** Well how do we know that?

**7** We've got her diary.

**6** How did you get that?

**7** Found it in her locker when she left.

**6** Why were you looking in her locker?

**7** Might have some good stuff in it and she's not gonna be using it is she.

**6** Anything good?

**7** Just a diary and some poems and photos and that.

**8** You should give that to her family innit

**7** Alright.

**12** Does anyone know anything about Sunland?

**10** It doesn't matter – if they ask we were all her best mate and everything we do is true.

**12** It does matter.

**10** Why?

**12** Because it's an international competition.

**10** So what?

**12** So someone is probably going to have been to Sunland. Did no one ever ask her?

**ALL** …

3 It's difficult to ask about something like that isn't it. Yano in case they've had some traumatic experience and they don't want to talk about it.

12 Okay. So what do we know from the diary.

7 That she's from Sunland.

12 Does it say anything more specific?

7 It's only got one entry.

12 Is it long?

7 Three sentences.

12 What does it say?

7 *"Dear Diary. I miss Sunland. I miss Mum. I miss Dad And I'm really angry at what happened there. Fable"*

11 That's shit.

2 What happened?

6 Something happened that made her have to leave Sunland and come here.

12 So if we're going to make this thing we'll have to fill in some gaps. What do we know about Sunland?

9 It's poor.

12 Are you sure?

9 My dad's from Moonland and he says Sunland is poor.

3 What's Moonland like?

9 Alright.

3 Why did he move here if it was alright?

9 He was a really big fan of Headball. Wanted to be near all his headball stars.

3 Weird thing to move for.

**1** Let's get back to the story. We've got half an hour and I want just to do it so we don't have to stay every night for two weeks.

**9** Sorry yeah. Sunland is poor.

**12** Yeah but we have to be sure because we've got to justify our choices for the judges.

**10** My dad's from Star Country. I just texted him and he said it's poor as well. You wouldn't leave somewhere if you were rich and it was all nice would you.

**1** I think she was poor. She had cheap trainers.

**6** Maybe she was rich in Sunland and just had no money here.

**4** Doesn't matter. When she was here. She was poor. She was on dinners.

**12** Right. I'm writing poor down.

*They write 'Poor' on the board.*

**12** Did she come on her own?

**7** Yeah she was on her own.

**12** Definitely?

**7** Yeah 100%. It says in the diary "I miss Mum. I miss Dad"

**12** She didn't come with anyone else?

**7** Well she didn't come with them. Put a question mark and we'll come back to it.

**12** No we've got to do this now. We need to make clear choices and go with them if we're going to win the competition.

**9** Look the evidence suggests she came without her parents so that means alone. We haven't got all day put it up.

**12** Okay.

*'Came on her own (?)' goes on the board.*

**12** What else?

1 People eat dogs in Sunland

3 People eating dogs?

1 Yeah.

4 What?

1 People in Sunland eat dogs

2 They don't.

1 They do.

5 You think Fable and everyone else in Sunland eats dogs?

1 Yeah.

12 Can we put a question mark next to dogs and then we can fact check it tonight? We're just getting the truth of Fable's story before we build on it with general truth. So can we put dogs down with a question mark? It might be seen as racist.

1 Yeah but if it's true it's interesting isn't it.

*'Eating Dogs?' goes on the board.*

12 Alright. What else? What about the temperature? What did she say that was like?

8 Well her skin was quite dark.

7 What does that mean?

8 That it's going to be hot.

9 Really?

8 Yeah you don't get people with light skin from hot places.

6 Don't ya?

8 Not really. I mean if you're from a cold place you have light skin. And if you're from a hot place you have darker skin. Why people from like… Pickland are really white and people from like… Hinistan are darker.

9 Is that true?

5 Can't you Intrasearch it?

8 Yeah.

4 Intrasearch isn't necessarily true.

8 How else do we find stuff out?

4 Ask people first hand.

8 Well we can't do that can we.

4 Why

8 Because none of us are from Sunland.

1 Can you Intrasearch about dogs as well?

8 It's not gonna have that down is it?

1 Why not?

8 Hive Mind isn't going to say that they eat dogs. And also it has to at least come from some sort of evidence. We can't just put something in about eating dogs because we think that's what people do.

4 Doesn't it.

8 No.

4 Look now.

8 Have you just changed that?

4 Anyone can change anything. We can't listen to it.

10 It's gone now.

4 What?

10 Someone deleted it.

4 Still though. Anyone can say anything.

12 Well. It's all we've got for now. What's the weather like?

**8** Hot.

**6** Yeah?

**8** Yeah that's what it says on Hive Mind

*They write 'Hot' on the board.*

**12** Okay what else?

**9** They do a load of weird dances.

**12** What do you mean do a load of weird dances.

**9** I mean she did a load of dances what do you think I mean?

**10** Why we saying that?

**9** Because of what happened in the canteen.

**5** Oh yeah.

**2** What happened?

**11** The dance.

**2** Oh yeah!

**12** How did it go?

**4** Anyone remember.

**2** Yeah I do.

*They sing a bit (note this is same as the music in Act Three).*

**1** No it was like…

*They sing.*

*Eventually people chip in until they're all singing it.*

**12** What was the dance like?

**2** Like this.

*She dances – taking the piss a bit.*

**12** Yeahhhh

*They all sing and dance.*

**10** Yeah write that down.

*'Weird dancing' goes on the board.*

**12** What about the food?

**2** Probably a lot of meat and stuff that grows in the earth.

**12** So it's a hot place, where people maybe eat dogs? They dance a lot and they eat a lot of veg. What about the houses?

**4** Probably not like mud and that but yano… Cheap. Tin and concrete. But it's dead hot so you don't have to worry about them blowing over. Like on the news.

**12** Okay.

*'Cheap houses' goes on the board.*

**12** Great and what happened?

**4** Well we've got that poem haven't we.

**12** What poem?

**4** The poem that she did for English

**12** Who's got it.

**5** Me.

**12** Why do you have it? **5** thought it was nice so I took it off Misses' desk when she disappeared

**2** Why?

**5** Why not?

**2** Fair enough.

**12** Okay just read it.

**5** *"I left Sunland for a better world*
*But Sunland wasn't bad.*
*It was just a place that was what it was*

*But what it was made me sad.*

*So Mum I know that it wasn't for you*
*But it might have been for me.*
*So let me know if you get chance too*
*What it was I couldn't see"*

**12** Interesting

**6** Yeah so what was her mum hiding stuff from her?

**12** What would she be hiding?

**7** Drugs?

**12** I don't think she would send her all the way because she liked drugs.

**7** Okay. Like what?

**8** Like gunge?

**12** Gunge?

**8** Yeah gunge? Sunland is famous for gunge.

**2** What's gunge?

**11** Like that stuff that comes out of the ground and makes cars go.

**2** I thought they made that in factories.

**11** No it comes out of the ground.

**2** Oh. I feel thick. Do they have in gardens?

**11** Some gardens and if you do you're rich.

**12** Was there any evidence about gunge in Sunland?

**8** Loads. Intrasearch it.

**4** You'll get some link to some weird propaganda website.

**8** Shut up about intrasearch!

*12 searches.*

**12** Wow. Look at this.

**4** What's the source

**12** Fetti Fetti a diary of a man from Sunland.

**4** Okay I'll let that go.

**12** But why would she send her here because of gunge.

**9** It's caused a big war.

**12** Is there a big war?

**9** Yeah.

**12** And is it about gunge?

**9** Yeah.

**12** How do you know?

**9** It's in the papers. Dolphinland and the Utopian Regions got involved.

**12** How and why?

**9** Basically: If the side they back wins then they get the gunge.

**12** How bad is it?

**10** Really bad. Towns get blown up.

**12** Are we sure it was because of that?

**11** I don't feel comfortable writing that it's a bit tenuous.

**12** Yeah we have to stand in front of people and tell this story so can we actually say that there is any evidence that anyone is fighting over gunge?

**1** It's all about gunge though isn't it. If all those reporters are saying it that's enough evidence.

**9** Yeah. Look her mum was hiding something about Sunland from her and there are battles there and she asked her to leave. We have enough evidence to suggest that her mum as hiding the horrible world from her and made her leave from that poem.

**12** Can someone Intrasearch all the facts about gunge and war in Sunland so we have evidence in case the judges ask? Who's fighting?

**2** Loads of people in Sunland – rebel armies and the government: Dolphinland and Utopian Regions are funding it.

**9** I texted my dad and he says that's true.

**2** Your dad looks like a fish.

**9** Why would you say that?

**3** It says that here too.

**11** What?

**3** All that rebel stuff.

**12** Where?

**3** Watcher.

**9** Told ya.

**12** Wow. That's horrible. Right. I think that's enough. Let's put it down.

*They write 'fighting' down.*

**9** But also write that it's people who are funded by Dolphinland and Utopian Nations for their own interests. Which is gunge.

**12** Okay.

*They do.*

**4** Hold on who's fighting?

**9** Rebels and shared belief groups and… Other rebels that don't agree with the rebels.

**4** Rebels vs Rebels vs Rebels vs Rebels

**9** Yes.

**5** And they're both fighting the government?

**9** Well they're fighting everyone. They're being backed by someone as well.

**5** Sounds like a game.

**9** Is to them probably – and the winner gets a ton of cash. That's what the Watcher says anyway.

**6** Why do you read the Watcher?

**9** Got the app; just needed something to read on the bus really.

**12** Right so let's recap. Fable is from a place called Sunland. In Sunland it's hot, they may eat dogs, they dance, she was quite poor. Because of violence (sponsored by Dolphinland and Utopian Regions) between rebels and the government for gunge. Her mum asked her to leave. Right?

**7** Yeah. Well all these things are true.

**9** Except the "for gunge" bit they're actually fighting for different reasons

**12** Why the gunge

**9** Because that's what Dolphinland and Utopian Regions get out of it. But the rebels fighting for something else.

**12** Okay. What?

**9** Far too complicated

**8** I don't think the bit about dogs is true.

**1** I do.

**12** Let's leave it with a question mark. So what happened next?

**2** Her mum makes her leave.

**12** Yeah but why specifically?

**9** Isn't it enough of a reason that they're caught in a massive war?

**12** You think her dad was killed fighting for the state and her mum made her run away in case the rebels get her too?

**6** Makes sense.

**12** Why didn't the mum come too?

**7** It's easier to smuggle a little girl than a woman out of a place where rebels are looking for you.

**8** Or maybe they were too poor to smuggle everyone out.

**12** Maybe

**9** Is the dad definitely dead?

**7** Well she carries a picture of him and she only ever mentions her mum.

**8** So what?

**7** Well if she hated him they she wouldn't carry a picture would she.

**12** We're getting ahead of ourselves. So are we writing down that her dad was a soldier and was killed fighting the rebels?

**11** Yes.

*They do.*

**5** Is it okay to do this?

**12** What?

**5** Make a play about someone's life without knowing it's all true.

**12** It's not HER life. It's BASED ON her life.

**10** That's what TV people say when they think a story will make them money but need to tweak it and still say it's true.

**12** We're doing our best. We need to have a real story and this is real. We're not saying it's "Her" story. We're just using her as the starting place for a story about immigrants coming here generally.

5 We have to be accurate! This is people's lives!

12 We can be as accurate as we can be but make sure there's still *some* truth in what we're saying and that what we're saying still has a wider point. We agreed that at the start.

5 I'm not comfortable. I'm not doing it.

12 Come on.

1 Why you doing that?

5 If we use her name it has to be true.

12 We're not saying it's true we're saying it's based on truth and that everything else in it is true so we're making a political point based on fact.

5 It's not fair!

12 It is fair!

1 Na she's right.

11 Shut up.

2 No you.

10 Alright let's just calm down.

3 Na don't call down this is a matter of respect. Like we can't just make up stuff and say it's Fable.

9 Look The Watcher says it's true.

4 Yeah well my dad says that they're just here to claim benefits and send to feed their shitty diseased familes.

8 That's racist.

4 He's right though isn't he.

12 Not necessarily.

6 He's allowed an opinion.

5 I'm leaving.

**6** Me too

**11** Come back.

**3** Na it's wrong.

**10** Don't be soft

**4** I'm not I don't even want to do a play about some little scrounger.

**9** Come back.

**1** Don't tell them what to do.

**12** Alright! We have to do this as a group. I want to travel. And we all do. Come on.

**1** Get back in here.

**11** You're ruining it!

**4** I DON'T CARE!

**12** Look. Okay. We all want to win this competition. How about we come to a comprise.

**4** Compromise what?

**12** How about we say, really clearly, in the title, what it is. And we make it really clear we're not telling Fable's real story but we're saying that we're using it as a corner stone to discuss the wider... Thing.

**5** What would you say?

**12** "This is a story about migration based on the real story of a girl called Fable". That way we use her as a basis and we can build on it to make our own points about migration without saying it's HER story. Okay? Anyone have any problems with that?

ALL ... No

**12** Great. Thanks. And we can't accuse them of being scroungers because the judges won't like it.

**4** Why?

**12** Because there's no proof of that. We have to be sympathetic. She was in our class, we're trying to convince them to be our friend, we have to be sympathetic. So where were we?

**6** How did she get here?

**12** Anyone know? Come on this is an important detail. It's the type of thing someone who knows anything about this stuff will know.

**7** She can't have just flown can she.

**8** Why not?

**7** Aren't they really strict about those things?

**9** What do you mean?

**7** Don't you need a visa?

**11** I think you can just fly here but then you have to apply for citizenship.

**2** Did she have a passport?

**3** If she had a passport she wouldn't have been taken away would she.

**12** So do you think she could have come illegally?

**11** Well you have to buy citizenship and she didn't have any money so we can assume that she wasn't going to do that and she wouldn't just come here for a bit and start school if she knew she'd have to leave would she.

**12** So you think she smuggled in so they wouldn't have to make her leave?

**11** Maybe.

**4** Wow.

**12** Can someone Intrasearch "how do immigrants get to Dolphinland?"

**5** Okay.

**1** It's mad really isn't it that someone would be so desperate for here. Why here?

**6** Good schools.

**7** Good education.

**8** Good equality.

**9** Health.

**10** Yeah there's a load of reasons.

**11** Nice. Fair enough. I don't like it.

**12** I'm just gonna put those things on the board.

> *'Illegal immigrants come here for Education, Equality, Health, Opportunity, Housing etc…' Goes on the board.*

**2** Probably mostly because it's just not safe where she was from. That's as good enough reason as any.

> *… And not getting bombed! Goes on the board too.*

**12** Illegal immigrants or illegal refugees?

**3** What's the difference?

**5** I think a migrant is someone who moves for a better life and a refugee is someone running away from something.

**12** You sure?

**5** Yes I intrasearched it.

**12** So which is Fable?

**5** Refugee if she's running away from rebels that are fighting each other

**12** Okay.

**6** How do refugees get here?

**5** It says here that refugees come here in secret ways.

**6** How?

**5** Hide in containers. Hire dingies.

**7** Hire dingies?

**5** Yeah.

**8** Do you think Fable came on a dingy?

**5** She could have done.

**2** I'd hate to be on a dingy.

**9** If she didn't have a passport she couldn't have flown.

**5** She might have had a passport from Sunland.

**12** Yeah but did she?

**5** I don't know.

**12** Right. No passport. Was broke. And running away from rebels at Sunland. It's got to be illegal hasn't it.

**5** Yeah but this isn't definite.

**12** All the evidence points towards it and we've got to say something.

**5** Why do we even have to say something?

**12** Because we do. It's important. Okay. Right. So. How would she have done that then?

**8** Well we're not an island so she won't have come by dingy.

**12** No.

**8** She might have hidden in a container?

**12** How does it work?

**5** Apparently they pay people to hide them in special containers inside containers so they don't get caught. They get taken out the other end and given a passport.

**12** But she didn't have one.

**5** No. She must have been screwed over.

**11** Do you reckon her mum gave her all her money then?

**12** How do you get that?

**2** Well if she was poor she must have done.

**12** Okay so can we say that's the way she came?

**5** It's not necessarily true

**12** It is true it's just not definitely true for her.

**5** That's not the point

**11** The point is that she left because of something and she travelled and it was hard and it was all to come here. Okay?

**10** It feels like a cliche story about a refugee.

**12** Yeah but maybe it's a cliche because it's true.

**4** What about the end?

**12** What do you mean the end?

**4** What about when she gets here? What happened to her?

**8** She couldn't speak english could she.

**1** No all she could say was lunch box.

**2** Wonder how she learned the word lunch box.

**9** Who did she live with?

**11** No one knows

**10** I think she just stayed with some people.

**12** What do you mean people?

**10** Like some nice people from church. I think she just rocked up and someone took her in.

**12** How do you know that?

**10** I saw her at church and remember thinking that they were just two randoms my mum knows that didn't have kids. Not even from Sunland. From here. No link there at all.

**12** Fair play. Right then. So Fable is from a place called Sunland. In Sunland it's hot, they may eat dogs, they dance, she was quite poor. Her dad, who is a soldier, was killed fighting local rebels who were funded by Dolphinland and the Utopian Government and her mum smuggles her out to here. To Dolphinland. Her mum spent all her money getting her out and she was smuggled in a container all the way and when she got here there was no passport. She went to the first Church she could find and some people took her in. She couldn't speak the language. She missed her family. Why did she disappear?

**9** They took her away didn't they. Came to the house she was staying in the middle of the night and dragged her off. They do all the time in immigrant areas.

**12** How we gonna end it?

**1** We'll end with that speech she did when she won that award in Assembly.

**12** Oh yeah I forgot about that. Does anyone remember it?

**10** I do.

**12** Can you type it up?

**10** I'll try.

**9** And we have to include the bit where we did the thing… That's what he'll want. So we say sorry.

**12** Okay. Great. This will win it for us. Can feel it.

**1** Let's get it right then.

**12** Oh. We have to sing a song.

**1** I'm going to write a song. For Fable.

**12** Okay cool.

*A bell rings.*

**12** Okay. Right then. Guess I'd better write the script!

**3** Are you doing it?

**12** I'll try my best.

**4** I just want to say one thing. And I don't want to sound racist… But. I just think that… This… Is all fine. But we're missing the truth. And I hate to be the one to say it. BUT. Really. What we're really talking about is that a bunch of people who can't afford to live in not poor areas smuggle themselves in here in the hope that they get a free house and they nick a few of the jobs that are meant for US. And take our health care and our… roadworks. And they do nothing. They just sit there until their kids benefit off our education and then they're scrounging. I just think that's the truth we have to say. I'm not scared to say the truth.

**12** So what do you want us to do?

**4** I think that's the play we should be making up. Because it's true. And we all know it is.

ALL …

# Act Two

## Old Anglby

*A Rehearsal Room. This time with props, a stage mark-up, and some costume. There are no sounds or lights.*

*The whiteboard is still there.*

*The actors carry scripts.*

**A** Okay are we ready?

ALL Yep.

**A** Right so these are the scripts. Shall we start?

ALL Yes.

**B** Fable was rich!

**A** I know.

**C** Why?

**A** Well only rich people can afford to send their children that far. Smuggling is expensive. Okay are we ready?

ALL Yes.

**A** Places.

*They take their places.*

Take a moment. And when it feels right being.

*They take a moment.*

**CHORUS** HELLO JUDGES OF THE INTERNATIONAL SCHOOL THEATRE FESTIVAL. WE, THE STUDENTS OF OLD ANGELBY, ARE PROUD TO PRESENT FABLE: THE STORY OF AN IMMIGRANT FROM SUNLAND TO DOLPHINLAND. THIS IS BASED ON REAL EVENTS. THIS IS WHAT HAPPENED TO HER IN THE

SCHOOL SHE WAS IN BEFORE SHE CAME TO OUR
SCHOOL BASED ON WHAT SHE TOLD US WHEN
SHE CAME HERE AND BEFORE SHE LEFT AGAIN.

Fable stands in a field.

It's big and it's huge and it's massive.

In the distance the sun beats.

The wind rustles through the trees.

And all around the sounds of peaceful Sunland stand silent.

That's very good.

Not far away people dance.

Not like camp fire dancing

Or like rain man medicine man dancing just dancing

Around a radio

To songs from Sunland

Nice songs

Happy songs

Songs celebrating the world and celebrating them and
celebrating life and celebrating how nice everything is.

Fable eats a banana.

**G** Hold on is that racist?

**H** No. Fable eats a banana.

**G** Why isn't that racist?

**H** Because everyone likes bananas. We can't avoid the fact that
everyone likes bananas because it's racist to a minority.

**G** Okay. Let's carry on.

**CHORUS** Fable eats a banana

And it's big and it's yellow and it's nice.

It's a nice banana.

No one is eating dogs.

Turning her head away from the music she can hear the tussle of the wind

The grasshoppers.

The Night.

Inside her house.

Which is a nice house.

To send your child with smugglers you have to have a nice house.

Only the rich can afford it.

And Fable, is rich.

Her mum and dad sit and eat dinner.

He tells her about his day as a doctor looking after sick children who were hurt in the battle the day before.

He is an army doctor.

**E** Imagine if we'd have gone with the soldier.

**D** Shut up. And she tells him about her day as a psychologist talking to men who have seen too much.

Fable listens in the way that daughters listen.

Fable wasn't really listening at all but one day she'll regret not listening.

And as they chew on their meat

The juices in the corners of their mouths

The taste of wine in their throats

**C** Do they have wine in Sunland?

**B** Course they do it's not like a backwards place.

**C** Okay. Could they not drink orange juice?

**B** Why would they do that?

**C** Because it might be a religious thing.

**A** Fair enough. Can we say orange juice? The taste of orange juice in the back of their throats. That's where orange juice lives.

**CHORUS** Fable's parents with the taste of orange juice in the back of their throats eat and love and talk.

The sound of the music from people dancing in the distance

And the smell of the roast chicken in their nostrils.

They're happy

They're doing something.

They're living. This is living.

And it's then

Right in the middle of the quiet

Of the happiness

Of the nothing

Of that perfect space of silence

That they hear it

The music stops

The grasshoppers go silent

And it happens

The explosion

It's distant at first

Just an echo from far away

Just a sound

An idea

But then it's again

It's closer

It's moving towards them

Cars

Sirens

Shouting

Men running

Babies crying

The sound of bombs

And cars

And shouting

Moves closer

Closer

Closer

And Fable looks out of the window and see's it all

The fire on the hills

The people running

Clambering into cars

Jumping on the back of vans

Screeching off.

Kids crying

Bags

People grabbing everything

People running

And it's then that Fable's dad grabs Fable.

And picks her up

And they run outside

Out into the night

Into the screaming

The sound of bombs

The sound of cars

The sound of violence running closer.

Fable doesn't know what's going on

We can see in the worry on her face

Her mouth in a silent O saying nothing.

Her father carries her

Her father opens the door of the car

Her father turns around and

BANG

Her father is hit on the head

A man with a pipe pushes past him

A man climbs into the car

"What are you doing?"

Eyes open and as she looks the man in the face

He's carrying a child too

"Shut up"

He says as he pushes past and gets into the car

"Where are you going?"

Away.

"Take me with you"

No.

"Take my child"

She can see the soldiers coming

She can see them shooting at no one

But hitting everyone

Old people

Young people

Anyone in the way

I'll give you everything.

And mum strips off everything she has

All her jewellery

All her money

All her everything.

And gives it to the man.

The man just grunts

And takes it all

And takes Fable with him

As the car pulls out fable looks back at her mum

Growing smaller and smaller

As the men close in she turns to face them

And that's the last she ever saw her of her mother.

As she drives off with a stranger and all her mother's money.

**A** Very nice.

**E** Hope that's enough to get us through school.

**F** Yeah.

**A** Shall we do the song?

**H** Okay.

> Fable dances in Sunland
> With the wind in her hair
> Somewhere in the distance
> The Sun is setting
> And the smell of dust is in her nostrils.
> Music is playing
> It's someone's birthday
> And the world is on their feet.

*Music plays. They dance. It's not quite… right.*

> All around the neighbourhood eat bananas
> And no one eats dogs
> No one here is rich
> But no one is particularly sad because they're not rich.
> They're sad because of the usual things in life

> Like death and war and love.
> And Fable dances
> And Fable dances
> And Fable dances.

**A** Very nice

**B** Yeah great

**A** Okay. Let's do the scene when she actually travels here.

**H** Okay

**CHORUS** Fable sits in the car for miles

Looking out of the window.

Crying.

Where are we going?

She says

And the guy just mumbles

Dolphinland

And Fable doesn't know it's a place

She think's he's being sarcastic

So she just looks out of the window and stares.

**D** What happens next?

**A** She gets to the station.

**D** Oh yeah. Fable gets to the station.

**CHORUS** And the man gets out and speaks to a man in a red hat.

Fable can't hear

But she see's him give the man some of mums money.

Then they both come over

And get Fable out of the car.

And the man says

"Go with him. He'll get you Dolphinland"

And Fable

Who's too sad to speak

Just goes with him.

And the man opens the back of his lorry.

And shows fable a tiny little hole at the back.

Tiny. Secret.

Behind all the other boxes

And he makes Fable get in

And she does

She's too sad to talk back so she gets in.

And the driver closes the door.

And lying there in the tiny space Fable needs a wee.

Quite badly

Really badly

And she holds it in for a long time

But as time passes it gets hot

And Fable gets sweaty

Her tongue dries up

Her brain gets fussy

And she realises she's been in hours

Days

She doesn't know because it's dark.

And time isn't a thing

So she wets herself

She lets it run down her leg

Fill up her knickers

But she's thirsty

So, so thirsty.

So she puts her hand in her knickers

And licks the edge of her fingers

Letting the wee quench her thirst a tiny bit

And then her mind goes

She starts to wonder

She starts to wonder whether she's really alone in this lorry

Or where the lorry's going

Is someone else in here?

Are they going to hurt her?

What happens she gets out?

All the possibilities of what could happen to a young girl in a strange place scratch through her head.

She gets nervous

Her palms are sweaty

And all she wants to do is scream

And run away

But she can't

Because if she screams one of two things will happen

She'll be found

Or if someone else is in here then they'll find her

So she lies

Crying in silence

Lying in her own urine

Praying that she can go be a hairdresser

Or a cleaner

Or anything

Anything in Dolphinland

Anything but a slave

All she wants is her mum.

And she doesn't know where her mum is.

**A** Okay great. That was good. Feels visceral. Shall we move on? We need to remember why we're telling it. We're telling it because for some people it's safer to hide in a lorry than stay at Sunland. That's the important thing. People leave and put themselves through hell to get somewhere better. To come here.

**C** Why is she coming here?

**A** Because that's where the men in the car was going.

**E** Yeah but is that the best reason?

**F** Well maybe she can have a better reason

**G** Like what?

**H** Like that's where her family is?

**A** Her family are dead.

**H** Yeah but she could be going to stay with other family.

**A** Na I don't like that. Feels too neat.

**B** Yeah it's better if she's going there because Dolphinland is better.

**C** Why is it better here?

**D** Dunno. There's no war.

**A** What did the white board say?

**E** Erm…

**F** Health, Opportunity, Equality, Safety…

**A** That's enough of a reason.

**F** And they're kind to refugees.

**A** Is she a migrant or a refugee?

**B** Refugee at the moment.

**A** Yeah a refugee. She's come here because she's safe and she can start a life here and do a job she likes.

**B** Yes that sounds good.

**D** Unless the authorities catch her.

**E** Has she thought about that?

**A** Let's say she's thinking about that in the lorry. What does she think?

**C** Okay she thinks she's going to find someone to look after her and work a part-time job until she can get a citizenship.

**A** Can she work without one?

**F** There's bound to be like a network of businesses that supply people who work illegally with work isn't there.

**G** Yeah. It's quite nice actually.

**A** Yeah. Should probably be kinder to people who don't speak like us. Don't know what they've been through.

**I** Yeah.

**A** Right. Okay. So that's settled. Let's re-write another bit in about her hopes and dreams whilst she's in the lorry. Perfect. What's next?

**J** The bit where she meets the people in church and they take her in.

**A** Oh yeah.

**K** No there's a bit before that.

**L** Her happy dance.

**A** What's that?

**L** The bit where she does a big dance about how happy she is to be here.

**A** Oh okay. Shall we do that?

*Some "Sunland" music plays. And Fable dances a "Sunland" dance. Everyone else films her on her phone. They copy her and take the piss – they become a bit… Racist with it.*

**C** And we've got to show remorse.

**B** I think doing it at all shows remorse.

**A** Great. That bit's really great.

**L** The judges will love that.

**A** Hope so.

**J** Yeah I like it. It's like metaphorical and also like… Truthful.

**K** Asshole.

**A** Shut up.

**F** What happens next?

**A** Well she's got to arrive here. Shall we do the bit where she arrives?

**H** Well we know what happens when the couple from church take her in and one of them not here today so we don't need to do that.

**I** No.

**A** Shall we just jump to the last bit? The end?

**H** Where Fable is in our school?

**A** Yeah.

**E** The bit where she feels things.

**A** She's always feeling things.

**J** I think that's a flaw in our play. She's not feeling enough things.

**B** Very good.

**A** Okay. So. Let's go.

**CHORUS** Fable stands in the lunch cue.

All around her people are speaking words she doesn't understand.

She doesn't know how she got here.

The kind people know a teacher and they said they'd turn a blind eye

They bought her a uniform

They got her on the register

And no one says anything.

She can say some things

Like lunchbox

And Mum

And Dad

But not much.

So most of the lessons are wasted on her.

She just sits in the back thinking about Sunland.

Wondering what happened to her mum.

And remembering her dad.

She eats alone.

A packed lunch.

The couple try their best to put in food from Sunland.

Like dog.

**A** There's no dog! No one from Sunland eats dog. Okay?

**C** Fine. Like bananas.

**L** Bananas aren't like necessarily a Sunland food either.

**C** For fuck's sake.

**I** Like… Juju.

**A** Yeah juju. Loads of juju. Okay. Carry on.

**CHORUS** And when she's finished the juju she goes out to play

And to her the playground feels like a war field

Like the one at Sunland.

The one where…

Yeah the one where that happened.

She thinks Okay

She thinks why not.

She thinks why not and she jumps right in with the boys playing headball

She knows about headball

Headball is very big at Sunland

It's big everywhere

And she runs

And kicks

And she's not good

And she joins in.

And the boys don't mind

Because Fable's kind of pretty

And it's sad

It's sad because she thinks that if she wasn't pretty

Or if they knew she drank her own wee once

They wouldn't want her to play

But this is the start

Every day she walks up to someone

Anyone

And she tries to join in with what they're doing

Until she could speak

With her voice or her body

And eventually

Eventually she could talk.

And she started learning

And growing

And thinking in Dolphinland

And a whole horizon opened up

She could be anything

Do anything

And maybe

Just maybe

Her parents dying was the best thing that could have
happened to her

Until they came

The men in the van

Whilst she was sleeping

And took her away.

**A** Nice. Really nice guys. After that we have the bit where we
did that thing. And then what we'll do is we'll finish it with
Fable's school assembly speech when she won the award.

**I** Shall we do it now?

**A** No let's save it for the competition.

**H** Do you think this is like enough detail?

**A** Look. We've got some stuff she said. We've intrasearched the rest. Nothing in this isn't true so nothing is going to be more true than this. Is it.

**I** Is that why she left?

**A** Well we can't say why she really left can we.

**I** Why not?

**A** Because we can't let the judges know what we did to her. Because if we're really honest – they'll never love us.

# Act Three

## Taraju

*The Space is now a stage. Complete with instruments.*

*The CHORUS get ready for the show.*

*A bell goes.*

**FULL MOON** Okay everyone. Beginners!

*The chorus find their places on the stage.*

**FABLE** *(To audience.)* Hello Judges for the International Schools Theatre Festival. My name is Fable and these are my friends from the new school here in Taraju. This is the story of how I came from Sunland to Dolphinland. I want to say a big thank you for coming to our performance. You asked us to create a piece of theatre telling the truth of immigration. There are a lot of truths we could not put in the play – this is one truth that we hope taps into many other truths – it is impossible to include all truths – only this one and we had lots of other truths in our previous versions that were also true – but this is the one we're showing. This is my truth. What actually happened to me.

**FULL MOON** Okay. And Q1

### 1.

*Music plays.*

**CHORUS**

*FABLE dances.*

> Fable dances in Sunland
> With the wind in her hair
> Somewhere in the distance
> The Sun is setting
> And the smell of dust is in her nostrils.

Music is playing
It's someones birthday
And the world is on their feet.

*Music plays. They dance.*

All around the neighbourhood eat bananas
And no one eats dogs

No one here is rich
But no one is particularly sad because they're not rich.
They're sad because of the usual things in life
Like death and war and love.

And Fable dances
And Fable dances
And Fable dances.

**MOTHER** What are you doing?

**FABLE** I'm dancing.

**MOTHER** Why are you dancing?

**FABLE** Because I'm happy.

**MOTHER** Why are you happy?

**FABLE** Because life is good today

It's someone's birthday

And I have everything I need

I have friends

I have family

And I have the best mother in the world.

**MOTHER** Can you shut that music off please?

*The band stop playing.*

**MOTHER** Okay we need to talk?

**FABLE** Why do we need to talk?

**MOTHER** Okay before I say this I want you to promise not to get upset.

**FABLE** How can I promise not to get upset if what you are going to tell me makes me upset?

**MOTHER** Well I need you to promise to try then.

**FABLE** Okay I promise to try.

**MOTHER** Okay. Your father is not well.

*Sad music.*

**FABLE** What's wrong with him?

**MOTHER** I think you should go and see for yourself.

### 2.

*Sad music.*

Fable walks in to her father's room
And the moon falls on his face.
As he breathes his breaths
The air wafts on his face.

Time slows down
And everything is still
As Fable looks on her Father
Who she had no idea was ill.

**FABLE** Are you okay?

**FATHER** I'm dying. And I don't want you to say anything. I just want you to listen to me. I want you to listen to me. When I die. And I'm sorry to say it Fable I am going to die. When I die. I want you to go.

Fable feels the weight of the world crash down on her
In her father's eyes she sees oceans of blue
And drowning in tears
Crystal drops on his eye lashes
And in turn her eyes swell with raindrops too.

**FABLE** But why?

**FATHER** Because when I die Fable. When I die we will not be able to have things. We will not be able to have money because your mother cannot work. And without work there is no money. If you are sick you will die. If you are hungry you will starve. If you have no job you will be homeless. And I want you to be safe. So I want you to go. I want you to go somewhere where those things are not a problem. I want you to go somewhere where you will be looked after. Please

**FABLE** Where to?

**FATHER** Dolphinland Fable. That's where I want you to go.

> And with his final breath
> Her father lent in
> And kissed Fable on the cheek
> Because leaning back
> And
> Like an actor doing his final bow
> Becomes himself for the first time in his whole life
> And breathes a final breath
> And closes his eyes
> And that's the end of Dad.

**MOTHER** Come.

**FABLE** Now?

**MOTHER** Yes Fable. Now.

### 3.

*Outside.*

**CHORUS**

> Fable's bag was already packed
> It was full of clothes
> And teddies
> And pictures.

It was full of love
That's the way to put it

It was full of love
And in her mother's hand
Was a small brown paper bag.

**FABLE** Is that money?

But it wasn't
She opened the bag
And it was full of bananas
Fable's favourite food
And there wasn't any dog to eat in sight.

*A car pulls up.*

**MOTHER** It's time to go.

**FABLE** But I don't want to.

**MOTHER** You have to.

And looking into her mother's eyes
For the first time
She see's a sadness
A weakness
A vulnerability

**MOTHER** Please go.

**FABLE** Why can't you come with me?

**MOTHER** Because we can't afford it.

**FABLE** What will happen to you?

**MOTHER** Me? I will work.

**FABLE** I want you with me.

**MOTHER** I will work. I will cook and I will clean and I will keep myself.

**FABLE** Why can't I do that?

**MOTHER** Because we want better for you. We want you to have a big job and we want you to have a big house and one day when you have a big job and a big house you can send for me and I will live in it with you.

**FABLE** But I want you with me now.

**MOTHER** I can't. It's you or me.

*A car pulls up.*

A car pulls up
And it's humming and brumming
And it's raring to go
Like horses in the stables
Urging for a race.

Fable is scared
She has sweaty palms
She has a worried face.

**FABLE** What will I do when I get there?

**MOTHER** You will call our friends in the church on this number.

**FABLE** I love you Mum.

**MOTHER** I love you too. Now get in the car before I cry. Please.

*FABLE gets in the car.*

**MOTHER** You will call me when you get there?

**FABLE** Yes.

**MOTHER** Okay. Okay now go before I cry.

**FABLE** I don't want to.

**MOTHER** Go Fable. Please.

*The car engine goes.*

The Car starts
And Fable looks at her mother for one last time
And it pulls away

*The car pulls away.*

And she watches her mother get smaller
And smaller
And smaller
And smaller
And smaller

Until mother becomes a dot on the horizon
A spec
A nothing
An empty.
And the journey begins

*Travelling Music.*

*The car (and FABLE) travel around the space.*

Fable passes fields
And houses
And towns
And all of Sunland
The whole of Sunland passes under her wheels
And her eyes see things they've never seen.
They see people eating dogs
But that doesn't mean everyone eats dogs.

They see life
And death
And tractors
And drunks
And drugs
And beggars
And kings
And queens
And big cars
And small cars
And big houses
And small houses

She sees everything
The colours

Red
Green
Brown
And mountains
And birds
And the sky
And trees
And jungles
And rivers
And streams
And everything
And she falls in love with Sunland
And right there
Right in that moment
She does not want to leave.
And it's then she reaches the airport.

### 4.

*An aeroplane waits.*

Fable has never been on a plane before. All of her body is shaking
She checks in her bag at the gate
And she worries that someone will steal it. Her palms are sweaty
And her knees are knocking like door knobs.
Standing the queue she looks at the other people. And she wonders

In all these faces
That look so happy
Or sad
Or nothing
Or dead
Which one of these won't be coming back. Which one of these
faces will never see Sunland again. Which one of these faces
will be starting a new life.

She wonders about their dreams
She wonders if their hopes will be matched
She wonders which want to be doctors
Which want to be nurses

Which want to be policemen
And which would like quite simply to be really really rich.
And as she has these thoughts she whisked along a corridor
and into a queue. And in that queue are more faces

More dreams
More hopes
More aspiration
More fears
More sweaty palms
More nervous sicks
And with that thought of sick she notices her own
Brewing inside her tummy
As she passes her ticket
Shows her ID
And steps onto the plane.

Fable steps onto the plane. She takes a seat.
In her seat her own worries cross her mind. What will the
people she stays with be like?
Will they like her?
Will she learn the language?
Will she earn enough money to see her mother again?
Will she dance?
She eats a banna
And the plane sets off
The plane takes off

Fable is sick.
As the plane takes off Fable's head is pulled back into her seat
The sheer G force is mega
And she's never experienced this
Her hands grip onto the sides of the seat
Her feet clench up in balls
Her breath sits in her mouth

And
She's sick.
All over the floor.
The lady next to her is digusted
She starts shouting
And all Fable can say is sorry sorry sorry. As she sits for next
three hours
The smell of sick
Lingering in her nostrils

*Travelling music The plane flies. The plane lands.*

*Two policeman are waiting.*

**FABLE**
Hello
My parents are dead in Sunland
If I go back they will kill me too
I don't know what to do.
Help me. Please.

**POLICEMAN**
Right little girl
Come with us.

### 5.

*MRS and MR OBI welcome FABLE.*

*Hello and Welcome*
*This is our house*
*We are your foster parents*
*You're welcome to anything you like.*
*We have tea and biscuits*
*And lots of nice things*
*Imagine that it's Christmas all the time.*

*Help yourself to bananas*
*Help yourself to lovely scones*
*Help yourself to anything but dog*
*(we've heard that you eat dog)*

*We don't eat dog in Dolphinland*
*Just a bunch of stuff lovely and nice.*
*This is your room*
*And this is your bed*
*And your uniform is here.*

*You'll like your new school*
*It's very very nice*
*And as you claimed asylum*
*You get to go*
*Don't worry about the language*
*You'll pick it up soon.*
*And don't worry about money*
*We have lots of it*

*It's part of being in the church you see.*
*Not having money*
*But being kind with it*
*And you're welcome to what you see.*
*Now goodnight*
*Sleep tight*
*It's time*
*for Dolphinland.*

**6.**

*Jungle music.*

Fable sits in the playground
With a packed lunch on her lap
It's bananas
She loves bananas
And its definitely not dog.

She watches the playground
And for a second she sees a zoo.
She sees boys fighting like lions
She sees girls preening like birds.
She sees weak children hiding in the shrubbery like moles

And strong ones charging like elephants
And she realises she's in the jungle
Only she realises she is invisible.
She stands up and shouts

**FABLE** Oh me!

And no one listens
The jungle goes on around her.
She sits on a chair and she thinks
She thinks about her mum and whats happened to her
She thinks about her friends
She thinks about her dad lying on his back in some hole
somewhere at Sunland.
A girl comes over

**GIRL** Hello

But Fable can't understand.
She doesn't understand the words.
She doesn't understand the gesture
So she says all she can say
She says

**FABLE** Lunch box.

And she hopes that will be enough
But the girl just laughed
And walks away
Leaving Fable all alone
And wishing she could talk
Wishing she could learn
Wishing she could live.

*Music stops.*

The next day Fable decides she's going to make an effort
So she goes home
All the way back to Mrs And Mr Obi's
And she asks for a CD
And they give it to her.

Fables goes into school with the CD in her school bag
She clutches it tight
And she's clutching it very very very tight
So tight that a passing policemen checks her bag
Fable doesn't know why
But later on she will realise it was in case she had a bomb.

She walks all the way to the gate
Past the group of boys who are being monkeys
And Fable doesn't know if they're being monkeys in general
or being monkeys at her.
She assumes they're being monkeys in general because she
still has the idea that people are as kind as they are in Sunland.

She goes into the shop to buy some lunch
And the shopkeeper raises his eyes from his paper
And watches her.
Fable doesn't mind
She think's it's because she's attractive
But she hasn't been here long
She'll find the truth soon.

She picks up bananas and some chocolate
The shop keeper smirks
So Fable gives a big grin back
And wonders how she would cope if she had no money.
In school she waits until lunch to pick up her moment
And whilst everyone is eating in the big hall

Fable sneaks in
And she gets out the CD
and she puts it on the speakers
So everyone can hear it
And it goes like this

*Music plays.*

*FABLE dances.*

And at first no one dances
Then eyes glance
And eyes meet eyes

And the people start to move

**TEACHER** Settle down

And with that the whole world starts dancing
Everyone is dancing
On the tables
On the chairs
Even the dinner ladies are dancing
And right in the middle is Fable
Doing a dance no one had every seen before
And it goes like this

*FABLE dances.*

And everyone starts clapping
And the whole school is watching
And clapping
And filming
And whopping
And Laughing
And Fable dances
And dances
And dances
And dances
And dances

And everyone else dances
But not like her
Everyone dances differently
Not nicely
Nastily
And they dance
And dance
And laugh
And laugh

And Fable stops
And everyone laughed at her
And films her
And laughs

And laughs
And laughs

**FABLE**
And my heart sinks
And I don't want to come back
So I don't
I go to Old Angelby
And the same thing happened.
Fingers. Eyes.
I have no potential there.
I lose by being me.

So I came here.
I came to Taraju.
A home away from home.
Where people are like me.
This is how they welcome me.
This is where I found home.

### 7.

**FABLE** I am here. Hello. And now I've been here for a while I see things clearly. I am staying with some people I don't know. I am miles away from my own family, I don't know what happened to my mum and my father is dead. The number my mum gave me does not work. I can't get used to the culture. I have to learn a new language and I don't have any friends. I miss my friends. I miss the dancing, bananas and the food. I miss the sun. I miss the wind. I miss the trees. I miss animals. I miss people that look like me. I miss people that sound like me. I miss not being different. I miss not waking up and being scared that I'll screw up and be sent home and I don't know what's there. I miss not having to save up to take a citizenship test. I miss being given a job on merit not favours. I miss people not ripping into me for being different. I miss not being guilty because someone is giving me money. I miss Sunland. And I know that this is what I will feel now for ever. I will always feel different. I will always feel guilty. I will always miss my mum. I will always feel like I am lucky but lucky and sad because I am alone. But that is part of being a migrant. Isn't it.

*The others hug her.*

**CHORUS**
Fable. We are all from somewhere. To show you are welcome here. This is what we have learned for you.

*They do a native Sunland dance for her. The one that was mocked in Part 1. It's amazing.*

**FABLE** Thank you

**END.**

**THE JUMPER FACTORY**

Written by Luke Barnes and the inmates at
Wandsworth Prison that signed up for Drama.
Directed by Justin Audibert

*The Jumper Factory* was a Young Vic Taking Part Parallel Production inspired by *The Brothers Size*.

It was first performed by prisoners at HMP Wandsworth on 8 and 10 May 2018 and was restaged at Birmingham Repertory Theatre on 31 July 2018 as part of the European Youth Theatre Festival. The production at the REP was staged with a new cast of young people from Lambeth and Southwark who were at risk of offending or had experienced the criminal justice system.

The Young Vic's 2018 Production of *The Brothers Size* explored the life of two brothers and their complex relationship when one of them is released from prison.

This inspired us to create a new production, *The Jumper Factory*, in collaboration with HMP Wandsworth that worked with male prisoners to explore the reality of their relationships with their own families and loved ones. Creating our response began by producing a special performance of *The Brothers Size* at HMP Wandsworth to approximately forty male prisoners serving a range of sentences. Shortly after we began working with approximately ten male participants aged 18–60 over the course of twelve weeks. Artistic Director of the Unicorn Theatre Justin Audibert and playwright Luke Barnes ran weekly workshops with the prisoners in which they shared stories and experiences to feed into this brand-new play, *The Jumper Factory*.

**Rob Lehmann**
**Participation Project Manager**

**Creative Team**

| | |
|---|---|
| Director | Justin Audibert |
| Associate Director | Josh Parr |
| Sound | Mike Winship |
| Participation Project Manager | Rob Lehmann |
| Director of Taking Part | Imogen Brodie |
| Project Assistant | Isaac Vincent |
| Project Assistant | Kwame Asiedu |

**Original Company
at HMP Wandsworth**

| | |
|---|---|
| Angelo | Malik |
| Billy | Shaun |
| Dave | Peter |

**Cast for European Youth Theatre
Festival at Birmingham Rep**

| | |
|---|---|
| Immanuel Adegun | Raphael Akuwudike |
| Jake Mills | Rushand Chambers |
| Pierre Moullier | Tej Obano |

**With special thanks to:**

Ash, Fredo, Neil, Nabil, Emily Giles, Steven Brien, Rachel Bell, *The Brothers Size* Cast and Company and all at the Young Vic.

**COMPANY** It would be really easy to stand here and say how awful prison is
That it's all full of horrible people
And that we're all really depressed
But the point of this is to say we're not just crimes
We're people
Living
We just happen to be, at this moment of time, in prison.

*

For the purposes of this we are not us
We are other people
We are a Japanese man in his forties that drinks too much and occasionally cheats at blackjack
We are a Mexican who absolutely loves drugs
We are a man from Ghana who robbed his own nan
We are Reggie Kray
We are Ronnie Biggs
We are Nelson Mandela
We are St Joan of Arc
We are Oscar Wilde
We are Morgan Freeman in *Shawshank Redemption*
We are that weird fella from *Mean Machine*
We are Johnny Cash
We are all the people you've never heard of as well
We are all the people who have been inside walls
We are not us
We are just telling a story
A story that is true without actually being true

*

I'm sitting on my couch
It's green
The type of green that looks like a dirty pond
It's faded
There's bit of it that's threadbare
It might have been the cat

Or maybe I just need a new couch
Anyway I'm sitting on it and I know they're coming
I can see them outside
I think about running
I think about going out of the back door and over the fence
I think about what would happen if I was on the run
I think they'd find me eventually
I think it's better to go quietly
At least no one's here to see
Mum's upstairs asleep
Kai's at her's watching *Bake Off* with Jay on her knee
I stand up
I go outside
I give myself in before they come to the house
I don't want to wake my mum.

\*

I am in a van
I can feel the road beneath me
I can feel the tilt of the motor left and right
My body tilts with it
My stomach sags over my trousers
My shoulders slump
I am heavy.
It feels like forever
All I can think of
Is Mum and Kai and Jay
All I can think of is what's going to happen to them
And what I'm going to miss.
I don't want to feel

\*

When I first walk in it feels daunting
Like I've crossed the first hurdle
A relief
Lonely

*

I'm in my cell
It's been a while now
Not that long
In fact it's only been two weeks
It just feels longer
Twenty-three hours a day is a long time to spend in a cell.
Getting used to only one hot meal and one cold meal a day.
It's a hard adjustment period.
On the first night someone threw a cup and it smashed an
officer's head open
It's hard.
But the biggest problem is my mind
My mind is imaging Kai with other people
Jay on someone else's knee
Mum growing old alone without me
I don't do drugs
But I would like to be doing drugs

*

My cell mate is an older man
He's nice
He's weird
But he's nice
He's giving me thrillers by James Patterson
He tells me he knows it's weird
He tells me he knows that no one reads these books apart
from old people and people on cheap holidays
but he tells me to read
Tells me it will take my mind off it
And I do
And eventually
Eventually
It does
I move on from James Patterson
I move on to school books
AQA poetry

John Agard
*Of Mice and Men*
I study
The old man helps me
He teaches me things
He teaches me maths
He teaches me everything
He teaches me to be inside my skin
I learn to be present
After a really really really really really long time
It stops the thoughts
It blocks out the voices
And eventually I learn to look forward to things
I learn to look forward to food
I learn to look forward to the gym
I learn to look forward to studying
I learn to spend my time in here preparing for when I leave
I learn to give into the cycle
I learn to breathe.
Then I remember my mum doesn't know I'm here.

\*

**YOU** Hello?

**MUM** Is that you?

**YOU** Yes it's me

**MUM** I haven't heard from you in days, I thought you were dead.

**YOU** No not dead I've just been working.

**MUM** Too busy working to call your mum?

**YOU** No. Well yeah.

**MUM** Where are you working?

**YOU** … In a Jumper Factory in the country. Staying on site.

**MUM** Is that why you've not been calling? No signal?

**YOU** … Yes. Have to use the landline and there's only one.

**MUM** How's the factory?

**YOU** … Very nice.

**MUM** Can't be that nice you've put fuck all on Facebook.

**YOU** I'm not on Facebook now Mum.

**MUM** Why not?

**YOU** Mental health

**MUM** Okay. Fine.

**YOU** Sorry I didn't say bye the other week. You were asleep I didn't want to wake you.

**MUM** It's okay. Except now, I don't know where you are. When are you coming round next?

**YOU** I think I'm going to give this job on the farm a year.

**MUM** So you're not going to visit me for a year?

**YOU** I hope so. I really really hope so.

**MUM** Right. Listen I've got to go. I've got an egg on. Will you call me next time you're not too busy?

**YOU** Okay. Love you.

**MUM** Yeah.

*

There are people in here that I think I wouldn't like to be.
Not everyone is like the old man
Sometimes people tell me things
Sometimes people tell me what they're planning to do when they leave
They're telling me about their plans

Their schemes
How they're going to find their fortune
And I think
I don't say it but I think
I think if they get this wrong then they'll be back here for a long time and I'm not sure it's worth it
I see the people that are here for a long time and they don't care anymore
Some of them
Not all of them
Not all of them by any means
But *some of them* don't care any more.
They're either dead behind the eyes or raging like bull dogs.
The Old Man says not to look at them
He says they'll twist your head
He says they'll make you believe in their schemes
Or worse they'll make you think that to survive you have to be like them.
He says that's not true
But you notice that people don't look at those people
You notice people give things to those people
You notice people are scared of those people
And you can't help thinking
You can't help thinking
You can't help thinking that life might be easier if you were like that.

*

I miss…
Being hugged, even just a touch on the arm
Sitting on the couch as Kai plays on the floor
Watching porn when everyone is asleep
Having sex right at the perfect moment when everyone feels it
Being around children; just seeing children play in a non-paedo way
Being able to bop to the shop and buy a Lucozade
Biting my Jay's cheeks and seeing her smile

Being with my family not even on a special day just on an
ordinary day where nothing happens
Feeling rain on my skin
Being able to walk late at night
I miss my mum.

*

A little boy comes in
He's not a boy but he is young
And he's quiet and you can see that he's nervous
He's got a slow speech and his voice shakes a bit
You don't know what he's done but he can't be in here for long
You watch as the guards lead him to a cell
And you see who he's with
And you know that's trouble
You know putting a man like that with a boy like that is not
going to be good for the boy
And after time passes
After not that long passes
You see that boy beef up
He goes from skinny to huge
He goes from quiet to loud
He starts fights
He shouts
He talks about schemes on the outside
He asks you do to things
He tells you he can make things easier for you
And you're tempted
You say yes
You hide things in the bank for him
And you get things back
You get money
And you know
You know
That he's not going anywhere for a long time
And you can see he looks smug
The old man tells you not to
He tells you it's not worth it

He patterns it for you
The Skinny Boy leaves you alone
And you thank the Old Man
And you're glad you're not him.

*

*A song where time passes.*

*

Time is funny here
It moves differently
It's sort of drawn out and short at the same time
People measure it out in places not years
Scrubs
Berwyn
Strangeways
Maidstone
Buckley
Time at this place
Time at that
I feel it gently
I see the end
I count down the days
I keep my head down
I keep my head down as best I can
I keep my head down as best I can but it's not always possible
I find myself living fortnightly
I find myself measuring time against the next visit
Fourteen days til the next visit
Ten days til the next visit
Seven
Four
Two
One
Fourteen
I feel the need for a routine to offset that

I feel the need for something to look forward to in the short
term
I look forward to the gym
I look forward to web design
I look forward to doing something
I look forward to getting out
Then
Just before it's time
Just before it's time for our time
Something happens
Someone sets fire to their own cells for attention
Someone gets beaten within a inch of their life
Someone rips their sinks and their toilet out of their cells
Someone OD's and dies
I've seen so much
And when it happens I don't care
I'm not concerned for their well being
I'm furious that free flow is off
And I'm stressed
I can feel the whole wing charged like lightning
Pent up energy
Banging on doors
Shouting
Anger
Rage at the loss of that one hour out of this cell
I go back to bed
And I look forward to tomorrow
I look forward to the next visit
The old man told me people had sex in the visiting room a
few times
I don't know how that's possible
I hope it is
I look forward to the potential of sex
I look forward to getting out
And I close my eyes
And I let time pass.
I let the moments pass
And it's really hard

*

I try to stay happy by feeling like I have created something today
Cleaning my cell with a toothbrush so it doesn't feel dirty
Play music and losing myself in it
Making a boxing bag out of a mattress and hitting it to death
Meditating and shutting everything out but the slowness of my
breath
Yoga; the feeling of my body relaxing into itself
Think of locking everyone else out of your cell at night not
being locked in
Reading and going into my head
Studying and knowing something better is going to be waiting
for me when I leave
Draw up plans for when you get out that will make you rich
that don't involve crime
Write stories to try and understand myself
Smoke and pretend I'm just outside the pub
I have sex.
Etc…

*

I am waiting to see Kai
I'm waiting at the table
I've combed my hair to make it look just right
She's late
I'm wondering whether she'll bring Jay
I'm wondering how much make-up she'll wear
I'm wondering if she'll make an effort with her clothes
I'm wondering if she'll wear that necklace I gave her
I'm wondering if she'll still wait for me.
She walks in
She's so beautiful

**KAI** Sorry I haven't been yet. I've been needing alone time to
process everything

That doesn't sound good
Maybe that sounds like she's not taking it well.

She looks like she's not been good
She looks like she's been sitting in her room hating you for weeks
It's okay. How are you?

**KAI** Fine

You're not fine are you?

**KAI** I am

But you're not

**KAI** *(venom)* I am

You're not.

**KAI** Okay I'm not. I've been losing sleep. I don't know if I can do this. I don't know if Jay can grow up with you as a role model. I don't know if you're who I thought you were. You've let me down. Mum and Dad think I should leave you. My head's been all over the place.

I don't know what to say
I tell her I'm sorry
I tell her I fucked up but it's not like she hasn't known other men who have fucked up before.
She pouts her lips a bit
That pisses me off
I remember her pouting her lips when I wouldn't leave Dave's party
I remember her flirting with other men to piss me off
I bet that's what she does now
I bet she goes out with her mates
And she thinks of me
And how much I've let her down
I bet she thinks of me and smiles at men
I bet she kisses men to get back at me
I bet she fucks them.
Have you been with anyone else?

**KAI** Are you kidding?!

I'm sorry

I'm paranoid
my mind is over-active here
Listen I messed up
It's not a long sentence
I love Jay and I'm more of a dad to him than his dad
I'm studying
This is the best thing that's ever happened to me
When I leave I'll have A levels
When I'm out I'm getting a proper job
This is what needed to happen in order for us to start our lives together
I love you
Being in here has made me value you and Jay above anything
When I come out we can start our lives properly
Do you love me?
I know you still love me
And she looks down
She looks at the floor like she wants to do anything but look at me
And she says

**KAI** Yes.

Tell me you love me.

**KAI** Despite all that I love you.

Thank you.

I'd like to see Jay

She's silent

I know that means no

**KAI** I want to be a father to that child I'm going to ask you again. Can I see Jay.

She looks around
She sighs
She does everything other than answer the question and then…
She pauses
Time lasts like what feel like forever

**KAI** Maybe

And that maybe is enough
It's enough to keep you going.
She shows me a picture of him in a coffee shop
He looks so cute
He's got a nice face
He's eating an ice cream
It's all down his top
He looks a bit fat
I decide not to tell Kai because she might get angry
I forgot about coffee shops
For a second it strikes me how far away from life I am
For a second I feel like a spaceman on Mars.
She has to go
We hug
And I go for a kiss
And she offers me her cheek
And that kills me.
And she walks away
And my life is over for another two weeks.

*

If I could speak to younger me, I'd say take all the badness out
of your world and turn it into good
Stop playing around and do some work
You can become anything, don't listen to other people, keep
yourself a secret and read
Educate yourself
Go to church
Make some money
Go to Scotland
Lead by example
Enjoy having picnics
Date. Loads.

*

Sometimes you wonder whether this is a reform prison or not

Sometimes you stay up at night and wonder whether it's a
choice to reform
You see people like that skinny boy who's now massive
He's on roids
He's in a gang with some big men
No one is saving him
He's just being left
No one is asking if he's okay
No one is telling him to work
It's more trouble than it's worth to have a conversation
And there's not many of them.
It's not their fault
Why would they if he's kicking off
If he's fighting
If he's causing more trouble than anyone else why would they
be kind to him?
You realise that this place is impossible to reform people
It's no one's fault
It's just if you come from a world where this is what you do
then being locked up with a bunch of people who do the same
isn't going to make anyone change
You look at the old man
And you see how lucky you are
You say thank you
And he says it's alright
And he opens his book
And he reads.
And I read
And I think about Kai
And I think about Jay
And I think about mum
And I think about how much of my ability to carry on relies
on them not forgetting me.

*

Jay comes into the room with wide eyes
Kai leads Jay over to me
He's wearing a sailor outfit
Why's he wearing a sailor outfit
That's such an inappropriate dress idea
He's asking why there are so many people guarding things
And why there are so many people waiting to see people
And looking into his eyes
And seeing Kai looking at me.
I don't have the heart to tell him
I don't have the heart to say that we're all here because we're bad
I can't
So I look at Kai
And I look at him
And I say

This is where Daddy works

**JAY** Do you mean you or my real Daddy?

I mean me
You don't have to call me daddy if you don't want to
I want to tell him his daddy's a dick but I don't
I want to tell him that I'm in prison but his daddy is actually in
Thailand with about £4000 he spending his inheritance but I
don't
I tell him to call me what ever he wants
And he does
He calls me

**JAY** Daddy 2

Which is nice.

**JAY** Where am I?

This is a factory
It's a factory and we all make jumpers
Kai gives me daggers
I have to go with the jumper story

It's too late to back track and have something good
For the rest of his life Jay is going to remember me as having
worked in a jumper factor in 2018

**JAY** What room is this?

It's the visitors' room
Behind me where all the guards are is the big room
That's the special factory room where all the jumpers are made

**JAY** Do you kill sheep?

No one kills sheep to make jumpers we just shave them.

**JAY** What does the big man with the tattoo of his own face on
his own face do?

He's actually a really kind man who makes sure all the
jumpers are soft.

**JAY** Can I have a jumper to take to my class for show and tell
so I can tell them all what my second daddy is doing?

I'll post you one
A really special one
A really special one made just for you
A Jay jumper

**JAY** Daddy 2

Yes?

**JAY** I love you and I miss you and I want you to come home soon

I love you too.

Kai smiles

**JAY** Can I come back and visit

I'll be here for a bit
And you're welcome any time Mummy can get here but it's a
long way away

**JAY** When are you coming home?

Soon I say
I look at Kai
I really hope so.


*


I'm talking to the old man and he's talking about running
He's saying that on the outside he ran every day
And you're asking why
He says it was his ritual
The biggest lesson he learnt in here is the ritual of getting up
every day and doing something
Finding a ritual
Others find God
They pray
They worship
They find an anchor in Churches or Mosques or Synagogues
or Gurdwaras
They find hope in Bibles and Korans and Torahs and Guru
Gobind Singhs
They work out
They run
They read
They find something that they do every day
They find ritual in something
But for others
For others, there's nothing
Nothing.
So they find drugs
Or what ever
I read.
A ritual
I get Enhance Status
I clean
The guards like me
I have a ritual
I do everything right.
I play by the rules that will get me out quicker
That's my ritual
That's my religion

*

*A song where time passes.*

*

*To be done in a different language than last time.*

**YOU** Hello

**MUM** Oh it's you how nice of you to call. How's the jumper factory?

**YOU** It's erm.. Yeah. Fine.

**MUM** Are you okay?

**YOU** No Mum I'm not.

**MUM** What's the matter?

**YOU** I can't… The other workers are watching me.

**MUM** Oh you don't have to be like that.

**YOU** What do you mean?

**MUM** You can't not get upset in front of factory workers to prove you're hard. They don't care they're factory workers; they all feel exactly the same being in the middle of no where.

**YOU** Yeah.

**MUM** If you feel sad you should talk to them about it. They'll understand. None of you have families there sure they're used to it. Listen do you mind if I go? I've got to finish the flowers before *Coronation St* starts I don't like eating after eight.

**YOU** Ok.

**MUM** Call me when you can. Love you.

**YOU** Love you.

*

Because this has been quite depressing we're going to sing a song

*They all sing a song.*

\*

I spend nights thinking about Jay with someone else
Daddy 3
I imagine in vivd detail Kai having sex with someone else
I realise that although I'm not in here for life, life is exactly
what's been taked away from me.

\*

People stop noticing me
I turn invisible
I've been good but I turn invisible
This is how they want me
Not human
Just a ghost that does nothing.
I do something stupid
I buy spice and a phone from the skinny boy
I think about calling Kai and Jay
I don't
I want to have something to look forward to
I get high.
Whilst I'm high I realise I am in debt to his mates
I've fucked it.
This can only lead to trouble
But at least for a second
For a second
I don't feel like me
And that's something.

*

**MUM** Hello?

**YOU** Hi

**MUM** Oh are you okay?

**YOU** No.

**MUM** Oh. I'm in the middle of dinner.

**YOU** Ok.

**MUM** Do you mind if I call you back in thirty minutes?

**YOU** There's no signal I'll be back at the… back at the Jumper Factory.

**MUM** I have guests.

**YOU** Okay.

**MUM** Don't guilt trip me you haven't visited in nearly a year you can't expect me to drop everything because you're in a bad mood. Okay. Relationships go two ways. You haven't made an effort to be in my life so I'm going to go and enjoy my time with people who have. I'll call you in thirty minutes. What's the number?

**YOU** …

*

The Skinny Boys fronts me because I owe him money
I don't have it
Asks me if I'm listening
Winding me up to get laughs off
I turn around
I think about saying something but I don't
But it's too late because he's here
And he's squaring up
And I stay silent
I want to walk away and tell him I'll pay when when I can

It's not much
He's not going to properly hurt me
He's doing this for status.
I turn my back
And whilst I'm turned to walk away he pushes me down the
stairs and laughes
Everyone laughs
a hundred or so faces drooling like dogs.
All of them
Telling me to do something
Telling me I'm a fanny if I don't
Telling me I'm a pussy if I don't
And I don't want to
But this pressure makes me feel
All the eyes
All the noise
All the everything everything everything
And I –
I smash a tray over his head
It barely even touches him
He laughs at me for being so weak
but the guards see
and just like that
All the good work
All the studies
All the privileges
All that good work is gone
Nothing good on record but me doing that now defines me
That's who I am to the authorities
Violent
Despite all the good I've done that's all I am
Violent
And that's not good for parole
No one remembers the good only the bad
True in here and true outside.
And the worst thing is that the Guards aren't Angels
themselves
Smuggling in anything we want

And no one does anything about them
It's just the way things are.
I am am now further from getting out
I am desperate
I am sucidial
I hate myself
I go back to my cell
And I start again
I pick up a book
Even though the old man is here I am alone
I have never felt this isolated
I have never felt this alone
And I count down the days
And I wait.
I wait whilst the world carries on
Whilst my family grow old
Whilst my lovers move on
Whilst my friends live their life
I wait
Here
With this old man
And I pay back what I owe when I can
I put up with the fighting
With the pestering
With people squaring up to me
And I walk away
That's all I can do
Isn't it.
And look forward to Kai and Jay.
And my next call with Mum.
That's what's keeping me going
That's what's keeping me from –
There's nothing keeping me going anymore.
I buy more from Skinny Lad.
I lose myself.
I know that I've messed up
I know I'm in here for a long time.

*

**YOU** Mum. I've been lying to you. I've been lying and I'm…
I'm sorry. I'm not at a Jumper Factory I'm in prison again and
before you say anything I just want you to know that I didn't
tell you because I'm ashamed of myself and I've fucked it and
I'm sorry and I love you. I want to be good. I want to make
you proud but I can't. I'm sorry. I love you.

**MUM** Have you hurt anyone?

**YOU** No.

**MUM** I don't know what I'm supposed to do.

**YOU** I don't need you to forgive me or tell me I'm good or
say it's not my fault I just need you to tell me you love me.
Mum? Mum?

**MUM** Of course I love you.

**YOU** I feel like I've let you down. I love you so much Mum.

**MUM** It's okay. I've got to go I'm going to Aunty Mary's for
dinner. *(Beat.)* I'll sort out visiting okay?

**YOU** Thank you

**MUM** Everything's going to be okay. I'll come and see
you and I'll bring some of those twiglets you like and your
favourite jumper. Bye.

**YOU** Bye

**MUM** I love you

**YOU** I love you too

*

Kai's not coming
I can feel it
She's late
And she didn't come last time

Maybe she's forgotten
I sink inside myself
I go dark
I think of being alone
I think of being invisible
Invisible to the guards
Invisible to Kai
Invisibile to Jay
I feel like a crab scuttling across the seabed and I hate myself
And then
Just then
Just as I'm about to give in and implode Kai walks in
And she's smiling
And she says

**KAI** Sorry I'm late
And she's nervous
She's shaking a little bit

Where's Jay?

**KAI** Jay's not coming

And I'm thinking why not
Why's she nervous
Has she come to tell me she's left me?
Is she about to say something dramatic and she didn't want
Jay to hear?

**KAI** Listen –

And that's not good
No one ever says anything good that starts with listen
It goes through me like a thunderbolt

Yeah?

**KAI** I need to tell you something

Great here we go

**KAI** Jay is besotted with you and I can't stop thinking about
how I wish you were with me. And I know you've been

working hard and your passing your exams. You are still passing your exams right?

Yeah.

**KAI** I know you're not in for that long but I just wanted to say... I just wanted to say that I want to give it a proper go. I just want you to know that I'm waiting for you. And I got you this.

She gives me a tiny box
Like the size of a stone
And I open it
And it's a ring

**KAI** I'm not asking you to marry me but I just wanted to.. Give you this to remind you... To remind you I'm waiting. And that I love you.

I love you too.

That's time
And she's got to go
Kai walks out and blows me a kiss on her way out.
And this tiny ring
This tiny little ring
Has given me hope.
Maybe everything is going to be okay.

**END.**